AF300707

WIKIPEDIA:
THE FREE COLLABORATIVE ENCYCLOPAEDIA

The unexpected rise of one of the world's most popular sites

Written by Guy Delsaut
Translated by Rebecca Neal

WIKIPEDIA: AN ENCYCLOPAEDIA FOR THE 21ˢᵀ CENTURY

THE SUCCESS OF A SEEMINGLY IMPOSSIBLE PROJECT

The free encyclopaedia Wikipedia was created around 15 years ago, and is now one of the most frequently consulted sites in the world. This success is all the more surprising as there was nothing to suggest it was coming. The collaborative encyclopaedia, which was launched on 15 January 2001 by the Americans Jimmy Wales and Larry Sanger (then 34 and 32 respectively), was initially intended to provide material for another, more traditional free digital encyclopaedia. However, the wiki technology that its founders used to make editing easier proved astonishingly effective, and the two men had the idea of creating an encyclopaedia that anyone could contribute to. This marked the birth of Wikipedia.

It was not long before the site became available in other languages, with French among the first. Wikipedia users from across the world could add to and update existing articles, and create new ones for a constantly expanding audience. The site's content grew rapidly: by October 2004, there were a million articles across all languages. Now, over 15 years after the site's creation, over 40 million articles are available, almost 5.5 million of which are in English.

Wikipedia, which has been managed by the Wikimedia Foundation since 2003, is not a commercial venture. Its operating costs are mostly covered by donations from individuals, companies and associations. Although the encyclopaedia's model was without precedent and seemed bound to fail, it has turned out to be an undeniable success, serving as a key source of information for users around the world.

KEY INFORMATION

- **Founders:** Jimmy Wales (American businessman and founder of Bomis, born in 1966) and Larry Sanger (American Doctor of Philosophy, hired as editor-in-chief, born in 1968).

- **Start of the project:** January 2000 (hiring of Larry Sanger).
- **Launch:** 15 January 2001.
- **Sector:** information and reference works.
- **Key figures:**
  - 2002: 19 languages; 21 000 articles.
  - 2003: 52 languages; 149 000 articles.
  - 2004: 107 languages; 440 000 articles.
  - 2005: 161 languages; 1.4 million articles.
  - 2015: 289 languages; 34.3 million articles.
  - 2016: 289 languages; 37.9 million articles, around 5 million of which are in English.

CONTEXT: ENCYCLOPAEDIAS IN A DIGITAL WORLD

THE ENCYCLOPAEDIA SECTOR

The *Collins English Dictionary* defines an encyclopaedia as "a book or set of books in which facts about many different subjects or about one particular subject are arranged for reference, usually in alphabetical order". Humanity has always instinctively sought to further the spread of knowledge, and this task has been facilitated by writing, then printing and finally the development of the internet. Encyclopaedias have appeared in many forms and under many different names over the centuries, before eventually evolving into their modern form.

The word "encyclopaedia" first appeared in English in the 16th century, but the modern encyclopaedia did not emerge until two centuries later, in England with the *Cyclopædia: or, An*

Universal Dictionary of Arts and Sciences edited by Ephraim Chambers (1680-1740) and in France with the *Encyclopédie, ou dictionnaire raisonné des sciences, des arts et des métiers* (*Encyclopaedia, or a Systematic Dictionary of the Sciences, Arts, and Crafts*) edited by Denis Diderot (1713-1784) and Jean le Rond d'Alembert (1717-1783). Diderot and d'Alembert's *Encyclopaedia* featured articles by some of the most prominent French writers and thinkers of the time, including Voltaire (1694-1778), Jean-Jacques Rousseau (1712-1778) and Montesquieu (1689-1755). The 18th century also saw the appearance of the *Encyclopaedia Britannica*, which is still published today. In the 19th and 20th centuries, encyclopaedias really took off and turned into commercial and ideological projects. Each major world power published its own encyclopaedia: the *Brockhaus Enzyklopädie* in Germany (1808), the *Encyclopedia Americana* in the USA (1829) and the *Great Soviet Encyclopedia* in the USSR (1926). In the UK, the *Encyclopaedia Britannica* remained one of the most widely res-pected encyclopaedias, and this is still the case today.

Alongside these prestigious multi-volume

encyclopaedias, single-volume encyclopaedias (such as *Quid* in France) also appeared with the aim of reaching the general public. Series such as the Oxford University Press's *Very Short Introductions*, which first appeared in English in 1995, also bear a resemblance to encyclopaedias, although each book in the series only focuses on one subject.

CHALLENGES FROM DIGITAL MEDIA AND THE INTERNET

Information technology developed during the 20th century, and computers began appearing first in offices, then in homes. From this point onwards, texts were not only stored on paper, but also on hard drives, floppy disks, CD-ROMs, DVDs, USB sticks, and so on. Computers were increasingly networked, and the 1990s saw the development of the internet and the World Wide Web.

Digital technology offered new possibilities and revolutionised many types of media, forcing their publishers, who were often from older generations, to adapt. The *Academic American*

Encyclopedia became the first encyclopaedia to enter the virtual world in 1985, when it released a CD-ROM edition (although this edition did not contain any multimedia illustrations). In 1993, the information technology giant Microsoft revolutionised the sector by launching *Encarta*, a multimedia encyclopaedia on CD-ROM. It was cheaper, more visually appealing and less unwieldy than the many volumes of traditional encyclopaedias such as the *Encyclopaedia Britannica*, which guaranteed its success. Traditional publishers gradually began producing electronic versions of their encyclopaedias, which were sold on CD-ROMs and then on DVDs.

These new forms of encyclopaedias made multimedia illustrations, searches within the text and updates possible. Furthermore, production costs for CD-ROMs and DVDs proved significantly lower than for the printing of multiple physical volumes.

The internet also presented many advantages, in particular the possibility of quick updates. Major publishers launched online versions of their encyclopaedias on a subscription basis; for example, the *Encyclopaedia Britannica* took this step in 1995. However, it remained to be seen whether their model could be adapted effectively to the internet. Like *Encarta* before it, the emergence of Wikipedia in 2001 shook up the encyclopaedia sector, to such an extent that some traditional encyclopaedias disappeared.

THE EARLY DAYS: FROM NUPEDIA TO WIKIPEDIA

THE ENTREPRENEUR AND THE PHILOSOPHER

Wikipedia was founded by two Americans, Jimmy Wales (born in 1966) and Larry Sanger (born in 1968). Wales came up with the idea of a free encyclopaedia, while Sanger suggested the technology that would make it such a success. Wales had previously studied finance, before becoming a research director at a trading firm in Chicago and making a fortune by speculating on interest and exchange rates. He developed a keen interest in the internet and created his own company, Bomis, in 1996. The company's main product was a web portal, which gradually began to specialise in adult images, and its chief source of income was ad revenue. Alongside this, Wales was interested in philosophy, and more specifically in Objectivism. He took part in discussion lists dedicated to philosophy, and even moderated one of them.

In this virtual environment, Wales met the philosopher Larry Sanger, a fellow discussion list moderator and internet enthusiast, in the early 1990s. Between 1998 and 2000, Sanger ran one of the most widely read sites on the Year 2000 problem. Meanwhile, in 1999 Wales had the idea of developing a free online encyclopaedia. This was an old passion of his: as a child, he had loved reference books, spending hours reading the *Encyclopaedia Britannica* and the *World Book Encyclopedia*. However, he could not bring his project to fruition alone, so he hired Sanger at Bomis as editor-in-chief of a new site named Nupedia.

The idea was to establish an encyclopaedia

whose articles would be written by volunteer subject specialists and reviewed by experts. What made this project original was the fact that it was free and its publishing licence was unlike anything that existed at the time: the encyclopaedia's articles could be redistributed for free according to the terms of the Nupedia Open Content License. The encyclopaedia would be financed by ad revenue and go live in March 2000. However, the editing process, with all its checks and corrections, was slow. Sanger then suggested using a new technology: the wiki, which allowed web pages to be edited easily. Wikipedia was then born, and was launched on 15 January 2001. The initial plan was that it would not be an encyclopaedia in its own right, but rather a tool allowing users to work on the articles that would later form part of Nupedia.

DID YOU KNOW?

Contrary to the founders' original plans, there are no advertisements on Wikipedia. This is a deliberate choice and is often emphasised in appeals for donations.

THE CHOICE TO BE "FREE"

When Nupedia was created, Wales chose to adopt the term "free". But what does this mean in practice? In modern societies, original works are protected by copyright, which lasts for the author's entire lifetime and even after their death (in the UK, texts only enter the public domain 70 years after the death of their author). A text, photograph, drawing or song can only be distributed with the permission of the author(s) or copyright holder(s), and even then usually only for a fee. In the case of Wikipedia, "free" does not mean that creators' authorship is disregarded, but rather that they tacitly grant their permission for their work to be modified and distributed without charge.

This is essential for a collaborative encyclopaedia like Wikipedia; anyone must be able to modify articles in order to develop and update them. Contributors to the encyclopaedia therefore tacitly give their permission for their text to be modified by other people. Until 2009, content on Wikipedia was published under a GNU Free Documentation License, before switching to a

Creative Commons Attribution-ShareAlike 3.0 Unported licence (CC BY-SA 3.0). This means that articles can be shared and adapted, including for commercial ends, as long as the original authors are credited and the content is reproduced under the same licence.

A DECISIVE TECHNOLOGICAL CHOICE

By choosing wiki technology to make it easier to edit Nupedia articles, Sanger paved the way for the collaborative encyclopaedia that Wikipedia would become. Articles developed quickly from the very beginning. Without this choice, Bomis's encyclopaedia project would probably never have got off the ground. However, Sanger fell victim to his own idea: as Wikipedia could now function without an editor-in-chief, the post was eliminated and he was forced to resign.

WHAT IS A WIKI?

Wikis were invented in 1995 by the American computer programmer Ward Cunningham (born in 1949). A wiki (from the Hawai'ian word for "fast") is an application that allows web pages to be edited with wikicode, which is simpler than HTML. For example, an internal link to a site can be inserted using two sets of square brackets: writing "[[Barack Obama]]" in a Wikipedia article will create a link to the article on Barack Obama. In 2013, a visual and even more user-friendly tool was incorporated.

AN INNOVATIVE BUT CONTROVER-SIAL CONCEPT

Wikipedia therefore became an encyclopaedia that anyone could contribute to. The editorial process is incredibly simple: somebody writes an article; the article is immediately available; other users can then modify, correct and update it. All changes are stored in the article's history, so that any inappropriate modifications (vandalism, incorrect or irrelevant information, and so on) can be cancelled and the creation process of each article, including the users who have contributed to it, is visible to all.

This means that encyclopaedias are no longer the exclusive preserve of academics and experts in a particular field. Anyone can take part, regardless of their qualifications, level of education or job, as long as they respect a few basic rules and recommendations.

However, not everybody agrees with Wikipedia's model. Since anybody can publish information on the site, there is no guarantee that it is accurate. In 2007, the French writer Pierre Assouline (born in 1953) described this process as a series of "high-speed errors"[1], while Pascal Rogard (born in 1949), the head of the French Société des Auteurs et Compositeurs Dramatiques (Society of Dramatic Authors and Composers, SACD) went even further, calling the site's contributors "anonymous cretins"[2]. However, rules have been established over time to improve the quality and reliability of Wikipedia's content. In 2011, the winner of the 1996 Nobel Prize in Chemistry Harry Kroto (1939-2016) even claimed that, in his field, Wikipedia is more reliable than academic textbooks.

DID YOU KNOW?

Users do not even have to create an account to edit a page on Wikipedia; clicking on "edit" allows them to modify any part of the page, and their contribution will be recorded under their IP address if they are not logged in. Nonetheless, there are some safeguards in place: some pages can be protected and contributors can face temporary or permanent bans if they fail to respect

---

1. This quotation has been translated by 50Minutes.com.
2. This quotation has been translated by 50Minutes.com.

the rules.

WIKIPEDIA'S EVOLUTION

METEORIC GROWTH

Wikipedia becomes available in all languages

While Wikipedia was initially based in the USA and written in English, its success soon became global and multilingual. Shortly after the launch of the site in English, other language versions were created in German, Spanish, Portuguese and French, among others. By January 2002, the site was available in 19 languages; one year later, this figure had more than doubled, to 52. The site currently has content in 299 languages (288 of which are active), although the English version remains the largest. In terms of number of articles, it is followed by Cebuano (one of the languages of the Philippines), Swedish, German, Dutch and French.

Number of articles per language
(in thousands)

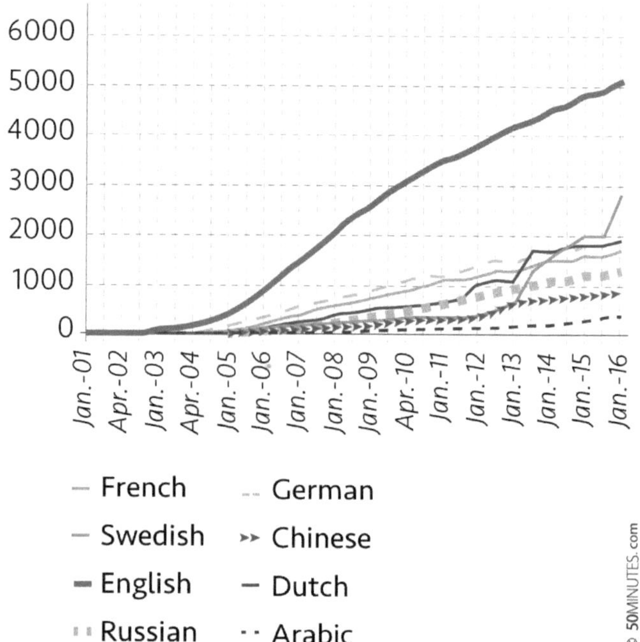

Although each version is based on the same founding principles, the different languages have a degree of autonomy, and it is the community that decides on certain rules and recommendations. There may be differences in terms of the admissibility of a given subject, the ways of presenting the information and the approach used. Articles on the same subject in different languages are rarely translations of each other: for example, the articles on Iceland in English, French and Icelandic will not necessarily contain the same information. It is also worth noting that Wikipedia is organised by language rather than by country; this means that there is not an Australian version, for example.

The essential rules

A project like Wikipedia would quickly become chaotic without some rules, recommendations and procedures. Wales introduced five founding principles, referred to on the site as "pillars", which cannot be challenged, while the rest of the rules are decided by consensus among the Wikipedia community as a whole. They are not set in stone and can be altered if the consensus changes.

The fact that there is no real hierarchy and the site is collectively managed by a large community can lead to tensions and may be surprising to some people, but on the whole Wikipedia's collective administrative framework runs fairly smoothly.

WIKIPEDIA'S FIVE PILLARS

1. Wikipedia is both a generalised and specialised encyclopaedia. By extension, this pillar indicates what it is not: a propaganda outlet, a newspaper, an indiscriminate collection of information, and so on. Users are also not permitted to publish unreleased study results on the site.

2. Wikipedia aims to be written from a neutral point of view. One opinion should not be favoured over another when writing about topics. This pillar is related to fact-checking and the inclusion of reliable sources.
3. Wikipedia is freely licenced, so anyone can use, edit and distribute its content.
4. Wikipedia's editors should treat each other with respect and civility. This pillar is focused more on the site's community than its content.
5. There are no other fixed rules. This final pillar encourages contributors to take risks and not be afraid of making mistakes.

The reasons behind Wikipedia's success

It is difficult to know exactly how this seemingly outlandish project became so successful. What inspired internet users to write about such a variety of subjects and spend hours completing pages or checking information? Apart from intellectual stimulation, on the surface it seems that they gain nothing from their contributions.

However, once the site reached a certain size, it became impossible to ignore. The increasingly widespread instinct to search the internet for answers to the smallest questions or doubts certainly played a role in Wikipedia's success. Furthermore, most searches on Google, the most widely consulted search engine, place Wikipedia pages towards the top of their results. The site has become even more visible since 2012 with the introduction of Google's Knowledge Graph: if you type "Charles Dickens" into the search engine, a box containing the first few lines of the author's Wikipedia page appears on the right-hand side of the results page.

The encyclopaedia's size is also undoubtedly a factor in its success. The 50 000 articles in the *Encyclopaedia Universalis*, one of the most respected French encyclopaedias, are dwarfed by the 1.9 million articles available on wikipedia. fr. The free encyclopaedia is helped by the fact that it has an unpaid workforce which can work around the clock and ensure that the site is updated quickly. This means, for example, that there is no need to wait for days or even weeks for an update to indicate that a famous person has died, or been appointed to the Cabinet, and so on.

THE WIKIMEDIA FOUNDATION

The creation of the association and its local chapters

On 20 June 2013, Wales announced the creation of the non-profit Wikimedia Foundation. It was initially based in St. Petersburg, Florida, where Bomis is headquartered, before moving to San Francisco, California. Wales transferred his site's intellectual property rights to the new foundation, which took over the management of Wikipedia and its servers, which are based in the USA and the Netherlands, from Bomis. This transfer indicates Wales's intention to make Wikipedia more of a charitable than a commercial project. The foundation now employs over 200 people and is responsible for promoting Wikipedia, as well as the other free projects it is developing.

Since 2004, local associations known as chapters have been springing up across the world to promote Wikimedia projects in their own country or region. There are currently 37 local chapters, with at least one on every inhabited continent and dozens more in the discussion phase.

Other projects based on the same principle

As well as Wikipedia, the Wikimedia Foundation oversees a number of other projects which are also based on a free, collaborative model.

Given that the founders' first project was an encyclopaedia, it is only natural that they would move on to another reference work, specifically a dictionary. Wiktionary was launched on 12 December 2002, provides both definitions and translations, and is currently available in 172 languages.

Wikibooks is a collaborative site for the creation of educational textbooks. It was launched on 10 July 2003, and now features over 56 000 pages in English. It is different from Wikisource, which was launched on 24 November 2003 and offers resources which are royalty-free, either because of their licence or because they are now in the public domain. The texts are therefore not collaborative, in that they are not produced by contributors, although the community can help to translate these texts. Wikisource currently has over 370 000 texts in English. Wikiversity, launched on 15 August 2006, is related to these two projects, and offers educational resources such as textbooks and classes.

A collection of free quotations, Wikiquote, was launched on 10 July 2003. It features over 30 000 quotations in English.

Wikispecies is completely different: it is a directory of existing species. It was created on 14 September 2004, and its content varies little between languages: as the names of the species are given in Latin, only the interface and featured pages change.

Wikinews, a collaborative online newspaper, is aimed more at the general public and publishes new articles every day. Given that the most important current news stories tend to be summarised on Wikipedia, some people have questioned how useful Wikinews actually is. Finally, the last of these collaborative sites is Wikivoyage, a collaborative travel guide which was relaunched on 15 January 2013 following a turbulent period from 2006 to 2012.

Wikimedia Commons and Wikidata

Two other sites, Wikimedia Commons and Wikidata, are separate projects, although they are closely linked to the sites outlined previously.

Wikimedia Commons was launched on 7 September 2004 and features over 40 million free media files (mainly images, although there are also some audio and video files). This means that all the Wikimedia projects can use files from Wikimedia Commons to illustrate their articles. The files are classified using different categories and sub-categories, and a description can be added in multiple languages.

Wikidata was launched later than the other sites, on 30 October 2012. It is a database which aims to centralise factual data, such as the dates of birth and death of public figures, the area of cities and regions, and so on. The factual data in the different projects could one day be replaced by a link to this database, so that if the information in Wikidata is updated or corrected, all the sites would be changed automatically. However, for the moment Wikidata is still in its infancy and has many detractors.

The Wikimedia universe

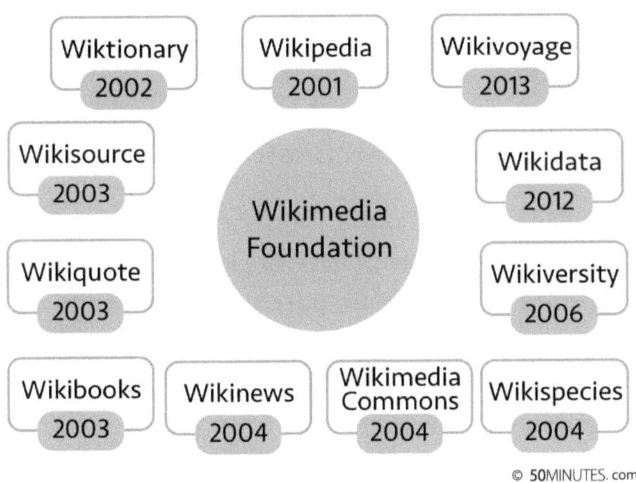

THE FINANCING OF WIKIMEDIA PROJECTS

Given that all its sites are free and do not carry advertisements, the Wikimedia Foundation is essentially financed by donations, which are solicited in annual campaigns. Around 2.5 million people respond to these appeals, and make donations of between $1 and $1 million. A range of foundations and associations also support the free encyclopaedia, sometimes with very generous donations. These foundations, which are often linked to American businessmen from earlier generations, include the Alfred P. Sloan Foundation, the Stanton Foundation, the Ford Foundation and the Hewlett Foundation, while the companies include the internet and computing giants Google, Microsoft and Apple.

The Wikimedia Foundation's other sources of income are the sale of licences in order to use the foundation's brands (in particular to Orange and Facebook) and the sale of merchandise carrying the Wikipedia logo (t-shirts, badges, mugs, and so on). Over the years, the foundation's income has increased significantly: from $80 129 for the

2003-2004 tax year to almost $76 million for the 2014-2015 tax year.

Income of the Wikimedia Foundation

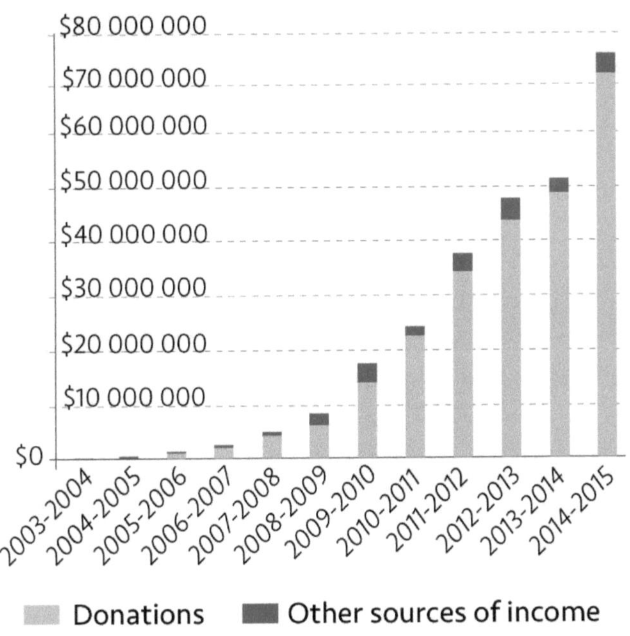

WIKIPEDIA'S COMPETITORS

In the space of just 15 years, Wikipedia has become a giant in the encyclopaedia sector, leaving its competitors struggling to keep going. In January 2009, the website Hitwise estimated that, out of every 100 unique American visitors who consult an online encyclopaedia, 97 consult Wikipedia, while 1.27 look at *Encarta* and 0.57 look at the *Encyclopaedia Britannica*.

Although Wikipedia is not the only reason some of its competitors have disappeared, it nonetheless bears a significant degree of responsibility. In 2007, the French publisher Robert Laffont announced the discontinuation of *Quid*, after 40 years of loyal readership, while Microsoft scrapped *Encarta* in 2009. *Encyclopaedia Universalis* and *Encyclopaedia Britannica*, its parent company, are still hanging in there, but only just. Indeed, *Encyclopaedia Universalis* ran into significant financial difficulties and went into legal redress in 2014. It overcame these issues in 2015 and began focusing on the digital education market, but had to lay off some of its staff. The majority of encyclopaedias have now abandoned their paper versions in favour of DVD and online versions.

Wikipedia's success has also inspired other companies:

- Google launched its own encyclopaedia, Knol, in 2008. It had a greater focus on authors and published texts either under a free licence or under copyright. However, the project never really got off the ground and was abandoned in 2012.
- In 2006, Larry Sanger, the co-founder of Wikipedia, launched Citizendium, which is similar to Nupedia in that it is a free encyclo- paedia verified by experts. Nine years after its launch, Citizendium has fewer than 17 000 articles, only 160 of which have been approved by experts.

WIKIPEDIA TODAY: THE LARGEST ENCYCLOPAEDIA EVER CREATED

WIKIPEDIA IN NUMBERS

By May 2016, Wikipedia featured almost 40 million articles, and 13 of its different language versions had over a million articles. Worldwide, over 62 million people have created a Wikipedia account. For the English version, there are over 31 million registered editors and over 125 000 active editors, meaning people who have made at least one change to an article in the last month. Since the site was created, over 2 billion modifications have been made to articles, and in April 2016, an average of 12 449 articles were created each day.

According to the web traffic tracking site Alexa on 19 September 2017, Wikipedia was the fifth most visited site in the world, the seventh most visited site in the USA and the eighth most visited site in the UK. According to figures published in the French website *Mediamétrie* in March 2016, Wikipedia was the ninth most visited site, with 16 710 000 unique visitors, equivalent to 1 738 000 unique visitors per day. The site is therefore a clear success in terms of visitor numbers.

WIKIPEDIA'S COMPETITORS

In many countries, Wikipedia is now the most consulted online encyclopaedia. It is far ahead of existing encyclopaedias, both in terms of number of articles and number of visitors.

China is the exception to this rule, as two rival encyclopaedias appeared after Wikipedia and now contain more content than it. Baike, which also uses wiki technology but is linked to a social network, is the largest Chinese encyclopaedia, with over 14 million articles. Baidu Baike, which features 13 million articles, is linked to a very popular Chinese search engine.

In Russia, where the authorities regularly threaten to block Wikipedia, a rival collaborative encyclopaedia called *Wikiznanie* has been set up. It was launched in late 2014, and as of 2016 had only a tenth as many articles as the Russian-language version of Wikipedia.

In terms of English-language content, Wikipedia is far ahead of its competitors, both in terms of content and visitor numbers. For example, although the online version of the *Encyclopaedia Britannica* is updated regularly, it still only features just over 120 000 articles, compared to well over 5 million on the English Wikipedia site.

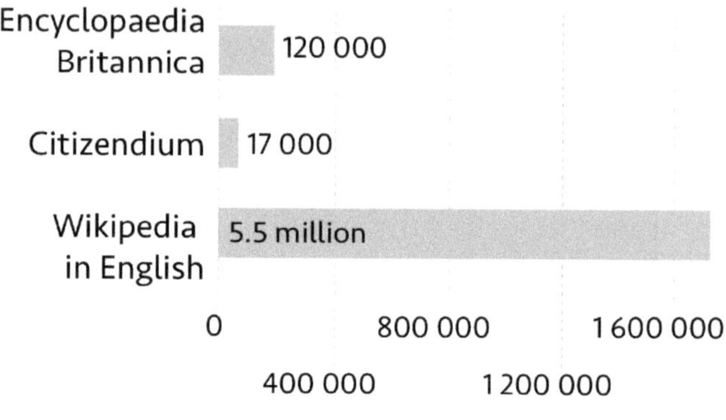

Nonetheless, Wikipedia does not consider traditional encyclopaedias as competitors, but rather as reference points: if a subject is present in one of them, this is a clear sign of its validity in debates about the admissibility of an article. Traditional encyclopaedias are also considered to be important, reliable sources within the community of Wikipedia editors. In any case, Wikipedia's aim is certainly not to drive sources like the *Encyclopaedia Britannica* to extinction.

PROJECTS TO HELP DISADVAN-TAGED POPULATIONS

The Wikimedia Foundation and the community of Wikipedia editors are motivated by a desire to share knowledge, which is why they have also taken initiatives to help disadvantaged populations across the world. As internet access remains expensive, the Afripedia project, which aims to enable access to the encyclopaedia through Wi-Fi when offline, has been set up by Wikimédia France, the Institut Français and the Agence universitaire de la Francophonie (Francophone University Association). Similarly, the Wikipedia Zero project launched by the Wikimedia Foundation allows users in certain disadvantaged countries to consult the encyclopaedia on their smartphone without being connected to the internet (and therefore for free).

THE CHALLENGES FACING WIKIPEDIA

The site's current greatest challenge is not so much to grow, but to maintain its current level.

In 15 years, Wikipedia has attracted enough contributors to become an essential site and ensure a certain level of quality. However, the site still needs to work to hold onto its volunteer editors, especially considering that heated debates can sometimes lead to the departure of people who have made major contributions to the encyclopaedia.

The next step is to overcome its shortcomings by diversifying its contributors in order to provide more information on subjects that are less well covered. For example, statistics show that most of Wikipedia's contributors are men, so it is worth considering how to encourage more women to get involved. Furthermore, there are fewer articles about Africa than other continents. Steps have been taken to remedy this discrepancy, but are they enough? Finally, the scientific community, academics and other elites are yet to be won over en masse by the site, even if multiple Nobel Prize winners have already praised its work.

SUMMARY

- Wikipedia is a free encyclopaedia written and edited by volunteers from all over the world.
- The emergence of information and communication technology, and the internet in particular, resulted in radical changes in the encyclopaedia sector.
- Wikipedia was founded by the Americans Jimmy Wales and Larry Sanger in 2001.
- The encyclopaedia's content, including photographs, can be reused legally by following the terms of the licence indicated.
- Wikipedia uses wiki technology, which allows users to collaborate on the writing of articles.
- The Wikimedia Foundation manages the site's servers, brand, and so on, but not its content.
- The project is financed mainly through donations, which currently stand at over $72 million.
- Apart from its five founding principles (known as pillars), the encyclopaedia's rules are determined based on consensus among its editors.
- There are other free, collaborative projects related to Wikipedia, including Wiktionary,

Wikivoyage, Wikispecies and Wikimedia Commons.

- Wikipedia is one of the most consulted websites in the world and the most successful online encyclopaedia.

We want to hear from you!
Leave a comment on your online library
and share your favourite books on social media!

FURTHER READING

BIBLIOGRAPHY

- Alexa.com. (No date) *The top 500 sites on the web.* [Online]. [Accessed 19 May 2016]. Available from: <https://www.alexa.com/topsites>

- Alexa.com. (No date) *wikipedia.org Traffic Statistics.* [Online]. [Accessed 19 September 2017]. Available from: <https://www.alexa.com/siteinfo/wikipedia.org>

- Assouline, P. (2007) Wikipédia, l'erreur à haut débit. *L'Histoire.* [Online]. [Accessed 18 September 2017]. Available from: <http://www.lhistoire.fr/carte-blanche/wikip%C3%A9dia-lerreur-%C3%A0-haut-d%C3%A9bit>

- Barbe, L., Merzeau, L. and Schafer, V. eds. (2015) *Wikipédie, objet scientifique non identifié.* Paris: Presses universitaires de Paris Ouest.

- Blondeel, S. and Thomas, J-M. (2006) *Wikipédia: comprendre et participer.* Paris: Éditions Eyrolles.

- Mediamétrie. (2016) *Audience Internet Ordinateur en mars 2016.* [Online]. [Accessed 19 May 2016]. Available from: <www.mediametrie.fr/internet/communiques/audience-inter-net-ordinateur-en-france-en-mars-2016.php%-

3Fid%3D1419+&cd=3&hl=fr&ct=clnk&gl=be>

- Rey, A. (No date) Encyclopédie. *Encyclopaedia Universalis*. [Online]. [Accessed 18 September 2017]. Available from: <https://www.universalis.fr/encyclopedie/encyclopedie/>

- Sawers, P. (2011) Larry Sanger on co-founding Wikipedia and how online education could change the world. *TNW*. [Online]. [Accessed 19 September 2017]. Available from: <https://thenextweb.com/insider/2011/11/19/larry-sanger-on-co-founding-wikipedia-and-how-online-education-could-change-the-world/#.tnw_ZiyWRCuy>

- Wikimedia Foundation. (No date) *Financial Reports*. [Online]. [Accessed 13 January 2016]. Available from: <https://wikimediafoundation.org/wiki/Financial_reports>

- Wikimedia Foundation. (No date) *Homepage*. [Online]. [Accessed 13 January 2016]. Available from: <https://wikimediafoundation.org/wiki/Home>

- Wikimedia Foundation. (No date) *Knowledge is a foundation*. [Online]. [Accessed 1 February 2016]. Available from: <https://annual.wikimedia.org/2014/>

- Wikipedia. (No date) *Homepage*. [Online]. [Accessed 19 September 2017]. Available from: <https://en.wikipedia.org/wiki/Main_Page>

- Zachte, E. (2015) Wikipedia Statistics. *Wikimedia*.

[Online]. [Accessed 8 January 2016]. Available from: <https://stats.wikimedia.org/EN/TablesArticlesTotal.htm>

ADDITIONAL SOURCES

- Meyer, S. (2013) *Jimmy Wales and Wikipedia*. New York: The Rosen Publishing Group.

IMPROVE YOUR GENERAL KNOWLEDGE

IN A BLINK OF AN EYE !

www.50minutes.com